Henry Wilson

The Republican and Democratic Parties

What They Have Done and What They Propose to Do

Henry Wilson

The Republican and Democratic Parties
What They Have Done and What They Propose to Do

ISBN/EAN: 9783337866228

Printed in Europe, USA, Canada, Australia, Japan

Cover: Foto ©Suzi / pixelio.de

More available books at **www.hansebooks.com**

The Republican and Democratic Parties: What they have done, and what th,
propose to do.

SPEECH

OF

HON. HENRY WILSON,

AT THE

REPUBLICAN MASS MEETING AT BANGOR, ME.,

AUGUST 27, 1868.

Published by the Union Republican Congressional Committee, Washington, D. C.

FELLOW-CITIZENS OF MAINE:

ONCE again the Constitution imposes upon the citizens of the United States the election of a chief magistrate. This high duty finds the people ranged in two great political organizations. Each has a name, a history, a platform of principles, a programme of policies, and a candidate. To one of these organizations the people, on the third of November, will commit the precious interests of the nation.

THE TWO PARTIES.

I propose to speak of the Republican party and of the Democratic party—what each has done, what each proposes to do. Holy Writ teaches us that the tree is known by its fruit—that man is judged by his deeds. During the past fourteen years the Republican and Democratic parties have striven for the mastery. Their policies have blossomed into fruits, their principles have ripened into deeds. By their fruits shall they be known—by their deeds shall they be judged. By the exacting standards of patriotism and of liberty the ages measure public men and political organizations. Let us summon these two parties before us. Let us apply to them the infallible tests of love of country and devotion to the God-given rights of man, by which they must stand or fall, before the living present and the ages yet to be. (Applause.)

In 1852 the Whig and Democratic parties contended for the last time for mastery. Then the great party, that had sometimes opposed a hesitating and feeble resistance to the aggressive demands of the Slave interest, accepted the humiliating conditions of the slave masters, fought its last battle, received a crushing defeat, staggered on, aimless and purposeless,

for a few months, and then ingloriously perished; thus fulfilling the prophetic words of the dying Webster, that, after that election, "the Whig party would exist only in history." On the 4th of March, 1853, the victorious Democracy received, from the nerveless hand of its fallen rival, the administration of the national government. In full possession of all its departments everywhere, sustained by popular favor, the exultant Democracy ostentatiously gloried in its complete subserviency to that all-exacting power which had dishonored, and then smitten down, its great rival. Alike in victory or defeat, the Democratic party had for twenty years bowed to the slave propagandists. At their bidding it had cloven down the right of petition and the freedom of speech, arraigned the illustrious Adams and censured the fearless Giddings; annexed Texas, "to give," in the words of Hamilton of Carolina, "a Gibraltar to the South," and "to add," in the jubilant language of Henry A. Wise, "more weight to her end of the beam ;" rejected the Wilmot Proviso, and given the slave masters the right to range, with their fettered bondmen, over Utah and New-Mexico ; enacted the fugitive slave code of inhumanities, and sanctified the unholy compromises of 1850; pledged itself to abide by that legislation, and to resist the renewal of the slavery agitation. This low bending of the knee to the dark spirit of slavery had seemingly won for the chiefs of the Democracy permanent power and the glittering prizes of ambition.

DEMOCRATIC EXTENSION OF SLAVERY.

When Congress met, in 1853, President Pierce congratulated the nation on "the sense of repose and security," and gave his pledge

JOHN A. GRAY & GREEN, PRINTERS, NEW-YORK.

that this "repose is to receive no shock during my official term." These soothing words, however, did not appease the lust of dominion and the greed of power. Those words of exultation—that pledge of unbroken repose—had hardly made the tour of the Republic, ere the nation was startled by the faith-breaking demand for the repeal of the Missouri Compromise of 1820. Lusting for dominion, the slave propagandists cast their hungry eyes upon the magnificent territory, lying in the heart of the continent, into which slavery was forever forbidden to enter — a domain which free labor, secure in the plighted faith of the third of a century, held as its rightful inheritance. Demanding that this vast domain, covering the pathway to the Pacific, should be opened to them, they bade the ever-obedient Democracy remove the landmarks of freedom, however it might "shock" the "sense of repose and security."

But this faith-violating demand for the removal of the landmarks set up by the Congress of 1820 to protect a region larger than the French empire when Napoleon gazed upon "the sea of flame," whose billows swept over the ancient capital of the Czars, stirred the nation to its profoundest depths. After a fierce struggle of four months, the faithless proposition received the approval of the Democratic Congress, the Democratic President, and the Democratic party. But that crowning victory shattered the ranks of political organizations. The Whig party was broken utterly. Hundreds of thousands left the disordered ranks of the Democracy. Nearly a million and a half of men ranged themselves together to recover that lost territory—to oppose the further extension of slavery and the longer domination of slave masters. Seldom, if ever, in the history of nations, has man been inspired by higher aims than then fired the bosoms of American citizens thus brought together by the needs of their endangered country.

In the ranks of this rising party gathered the noblest spirits of the land; the Christian, upon whose vision flashed the imperative injunction of Holy Writ—break every yoke—undo the heavy burden—let the oppressed go free; the Scholar, who found, in the pages of the mighty dead of all ages, testimonies that deepened his convictions and quickened his zeal for the equal rights of struggling humanity; the Philanthropist, who saw, as he gazed into the grave of perished nations, that slavery poisoned their lives, and hastened their decline and death. Into this new organization came also the veteran Abolitionist, who, with Brougham, scouted "the wild and guilty fantasy that man can hold property in man," and who had proclaimed emancipation to be the duty of the master and the right of the slave, when he "held," in the words of Whittier, "property, liberty, and life itself at the mercy of lawless mobs;" the Free Soiler, who believed with William Ellery Channing, that to extend slavery "we invite the scorn, indignation, and abhorrence of the world;" the Whig, who believed with Adams that "slavery taints the very sources of moral principle;" with Clay, that "it is a grievous wrong no contingency can make right;" with Webster, that "it is

opposed to the whole spirit of the Gospel, and to the teachings of Jesus Christ:" and the Democrat, in whose ear lingered the deathless words of Jefferson and Madison, the Democratic leaders of our earlier times. This political organization, born of the holier aspirations of the people, became the Republican party. Is it matter for wonder, then, that between this party—the product of the highest ideas of Christian civilization of the Western World—and that party, inheriting the maddening passions, cruel prejudices, and disorganizing theories that nurture slavery and develop its power, there should have been, during these fourteen years, conflicts of ideas, principles, and policies which have shaken society to its foundation?

Ere this party could make a national organization or find a name, it was forced into action. To silence the protests of free labor, whose inheritance they were despoiling, the Democratic chiefs beguiled the people with the illusions of "squatter sovereignty." The people of the Territories were to be left "perfectly free to vote slavery down or vote slavery up." But the men who had ruthlessly violated the plighted faith of the nation did not hesitate to violate their own pledges to the toiling men who were striving to make homes and found the institutions of freedom beyond the Missouri. The slave propagandists, so long accustomed to unquestioned supremacy, were startled by the grand uprising of the hosts of freedom, and the determined purpose of free labor to recover its lost inheritance. (Loud applause.) They saw that, unless they could thwart the champions of free labor, their criminal victory was but a barren triumph.

They sounded the alarm. They bade their brutal tools invade Kansas, seize ballot-boxes, elect legislatures, enact slave codes, silence free speech, and bathe its soil with blood. Faithfully did the Democratic party toil in Kansas, in Congress, in the Executive departments, everywhere, to execute these decrees. Hordes of border ruffians rushed into the territory, usurped the government, enacted slave codes, robbed, burned, and murdered. In Congress their champions were hardly less brutal than in the wilds of that distant region. Charles Sumner portrayed their crimes, and he was smitten down on the floor of the Senate by a "brutal, murderous, and cowardly assault." Reeder and Walker and Stanton, striving to right the wrongs of the Free State settlers, were removed by the Democratic administrations of Pierce and Buchanan. In obedience to imperative demands, the weak and wicked administration of James Buchanan strove to force through Congress, by the corrupting appliances of Executive patronage, the Lecompton constitution. Defeated in these efforts, the Democracy successfully resisted her admission under her free constitution, until its power was broken by the treason and secession of its Southern chiefs. (A voice: "That's so.")

To the faith-breaking abrogation of the Missouri prohibition, to the border ruffian foray, to the slave codes, to the lawlessness that bathed that beautiful land in blood, to the removals of Reeder and Walker and Stanton, to

3

the Lecompton constitution, to each and all of these, the Republican party persistently opposed every means sanctioned by reason, by humanity, and religion ; and this untiring purpose, this persistent constancy, baffled the efforts of the Democracy, broke the line of the advancing slave power, and gave to the Union a new Commonwealth radiant with liberty. Kansas, assured to freedom, was the first fruits of the Republican party, whose history now glitters with brilliant deeds and glorious achievements.

When, in 1856, lawless violence reddened the sods with the blood, and illumined the skies with the burning cabins, of the Free State settlers, the Democratic party met in national convention, reaffirmed its fatal policy, nominated James Buchanan, and went into the election completely dominated by the slave power. Well might the impulsive Keitt boastingly exclaim, "The South has the general control of the Democratic party." The Republican party, too, met in national convention, denied the authority of Congress, or any territorial legislature, or any other power, to give legal existence to slavery in the Territories, asserted the power and the duty of Congress to prohibit it in the Territories, and proclaimed its belief, with the fathers, in the self-evident truth that all men are created equal. (Cries of "Good.")

THE ISSUES JOINED.

The issues were clearly defined and distinctly presented. The Republican party, inspired by patriotism and liberty, appealed to the people, by all that was noblest and holiest in humanity, to rescue the endangered nation. The Democratic party, guided by the disciples of Calhoun, upon whose dazzled vision loomed up in the near future a confederation of slaveholding commonwealths, raised the startling war-cry of disunion. Slidell, the master-spirit of the Buchanan canvass, proclaimed, " If Fremont should be elected, the Union would be dissolved." Mason was for "the separation of the States." Butler declared, if Fremont should be chosen, " I should advise my legislature to go at the tap of the drum." Toombs announced that, if Fremont was elected, "the Union would be dissolved, and ought to be dissolved." Keitt emphatically asserted that, " If Fremont is elected, adherence to the Union is treason to liberty," that "the Southern man, who will submit to his election, is a traitor and a coward." Brooks, who would not " post a sentinel who would not swear that slavery was right," was, if Fremont should be elected, " for the people rising in their majesty, above the laws and the leaders, taking the power into their own hands, going by concert, or not by concert, and laying the strong arm of Southern freemen upon the treasury and the archives of the government." Henry A. Wise, who would " introduce slavery into the heart of the North," was ready to seize the Harper's Ferry Arsenal, the Norfolk Navy Yard, to march on Washington with twenty thousand men, and to put the military forces of Virginia upon a war footing, so that her chivalry might "hew their bright way through all opposing legions." The air was burdened with the seditious, revolution-

ary, and treasonable utterances of Democratic orators and presses.

While these menaces were falling thick and fast upon the ear of the nation, the Republicans everywhere avowed their unabated attachment to their country and their government. The crimes against Kansas, the mobbings, scourgings, and lynchings in the South, did not shake their steady faith in Republican institutions, while they intensified their love of country. Test the Republican party in its first great national struggle, by the standard of patriotism. Does not that unerring test reveal the glorious fact that it was loyal in thought, word, and deed ? Tested by that standard, was not the Democratic party more than tainted with disloyalty ?

DEMOCRATIC DISUNION THREATS.

In the contest between the vital forces of slavery extension and slavery restriction, the Republicans accepted as their faith the creed of human equality. They turned for instruction and guidance to the great men of the South of our earlier times. They saw, with Washington, "the direful effects of slavery." They believed, with Madison, that it " was a dreadful calamity ;" with Monroe, that " it preyed upon the vitals of the Union ;" with George Mason, that " it brought the curse of Heaven upon a country ;" and, with Jefferson, they "trembled when they remembered that God is just and that his justice will not sleep forever." They saw that millions of acres, of the finest soil of the western world, were, in the words of one of the sons of the Old Dominion, " barren, desolate, and seared, as if by the avenging hand of heaven." They saw, too, that slavery had not only scarred the fields of the South, but that it had more deeply scarred the face of humanity, that its ruinous power was visibly written on the foreheads of the bondmen, and on the foreheads, too, of millions of our own proud race. They saw that it dishonored labor, created, in the words of Olmsted, " a devilish, undisguised, and recognized contempt for all humbler classes." Accepting these teachings, and realizing the measureless evils and sumless agonies of slavery, they strove, with unflagging resolution, to consecrate the territorial possessions of the Republic —all it then possessed and all that it might thereafter acquire—to freedom and free institutions.

In this great contest of 1856 the Democratic party disowned the creed of the fathers, and accepted the theories of the school of Calhoun. The Declaration of Independence was pronounced false and fallacious, and free society a " failure," " a conglomeration of greasy mechanics, filthy operatives, small-fisted farmers," not " fit associates for Southern gentlemen's body servants." These sentiments, so contemptuous of the toiling millions, passed unrebuked by Northern Democrats, who followed their leaders with craven soul and fettered lip. Tested by the standard of Liberty, was not the Republican party bravely, nobly, righteously right ? Was not the Democratic party cowardly, and ignobly, wickedly wrong ? (Voices : " Yes, yes.") In the lights of to-day what friend of human rights, the wide world over, would blur or stain that bright record of Republican fidelity to the sacred cause of human nature? Who would not efface, if he could, for the honor of his race, that dark and ever darkening record of Democratic apostasy to freedom?

Although the Democracy came out of the contest of 1856 victorious, its chiefs could not fail to see that it escaped defeat by the timidity of that conservatism which shrank appalled before revolutionary menaces. In that grand uprising, in that doubtful struggle on the prairies of Kansas, the slave masters saw their waning power. Coming to the realization that every enduring principle of national policy, every permanent interest of the people must continue to be hostile to their ascendency, conscious that they could not much longer retain power, they addressed themselves, with earnest purpose, to the consolidation of the South, appealing to Southern interest, and firing Southern ambition with the idea of a splendid empire, commanding, with its tropical productions and its millions of slaves, the commerce of the world. They fired the Southern heart, brain, and soul, with malignant hate and bitter scorn of Yankee institutions, with lofty contempt of free society, and haughty defiance of the national government. (Cries of " Shame.") Resolved, in the words of Calhoun, whose disciples they were, " to force the slavery issue upon the North," they wrung from the Supreme Court the Dred Scott *dicta.* They bade New-Mexico enact a slave code, and also a code for the servitude of white laboring men. They sent Walker to Central America to win territory, " for," in the words of Brown of Mississippi, " the planting and spreading of slavery," and they sighed for Cuba, which they could not clutch.

REBEL YELLS IN CONGRESS.

When the nation was looking forward to the approaching presidential election of 1860, these Southern Democratic leaders, frenzied with the fanaticism of slavery, came into the 36th Congress haughtily threatening the dismemberment of the Union, if the people should choose a chief magistrate opposed to slavery extension, protection, and domination. The halls of Congress again rang with the revolutionary menaces of incipient treason. Jefferson Davis, foremost among that unhallowed combination, had spent the summer of 1859 in the North. Returning to Mississippi in the autumn of that year with assurances, that, if the slavery contest came to blows, " the Northern Democrats would throttle the Republicans in their tracks," he advised the people of the South to turn their old muskets into Minie rifles, prepare powder, shot, and shell ; for if the Republicans should elect the next President, he was " for asserting the independence of Mississippi, for the immediate withdrawal from the Union." Brown, not to be outdone by his rival, " would make a refusal to acquire territory, because it was to be slave territory, a cause of disunion." Clay declared that Alabama, " if she is not recreant to all that State pride, integrity, and duty demand, will

never submit to your authority." Toombs called upon Georgia to " listen to no vain babblings, no treacherous jargon about overt acts ; the enemy is at your door, wait not for him at the hearthstone, meet him at the door-sill." Iverson would not even submit to the election of John Sherman for speaker. " In that event," he exclaimed, " I would walk out of this Capitol, I would counsel my constituents instantly to dissolve all political ties with a party and a people who thus trample on our rights." Clingman would wait for no overt act, for " no other ' overt act ' can so imperatively demand resistance on our part as the simple election of their candidate."

The hall of the House echoed with these seditious mutterings of the disloyal Democracy. Democratic office-holders, thronging the galleries, applauded the guilty menace to ' shiver the Union from turret to foundation stone." Slavery, disloyal in every fibre of its being, seemed to have infused its malignant passion, its deadliest poison, into the brain, the soul, the heart of the Democracy. Their record, for that winter, is a record of shameless apostasy to the country, to the liberties of the people, to the civilization of the age. In that time of Democratic apostasy, the Republicans maintained with unflinching firmness the unity of the Republic, the authority of the government, and the rights of mankind. Whoever reads the records of that day will realize that Republicanism was inspired by the generous, elevating, ennobling spirit of Liberty, and that the Democracy was dominated by the narrow, vulgar, brutal barbarism of slavery.

THE STRUGGLE OF 1860.

In the Presidential election of 1860, the Democracy, that had borne the banners of slavery, won its victories, and shared its crimes, was severed into two factions ; but these factions struggled right on with equal subserviency to their old masters. One faction proclaimed, in the language of President Buchanan, that, " by virtue of the Constitution the master has the right to take his slave into the Territories as property and have it protected there under the Federal Constitution," that " neither Congress nor the Territorial legislature, nor any human power has any authority to annul or impair this vested right." This section of the Democracy, thus resolved to force the nation to accept the creeds, acknowledge the sway, and bear the crimes of slave propagandism, nominated John C. Breckinridge. This slave code section went into the canvass breathing out threats of civil war. They would permit the Republicans to win power only " over the prostrate bodies of the slain sons of the South." The squatter sovereignty section, timidly shrinking from the logic of its " great principle," submitted to the Supreme Court, which had already made the Dred Scott decision, the transcendent question, whether a million and a half of the square miles of the Republic should be gladdened by the footsteps and beautified by the hand of free labor, or seared and blasted by the feudal curse, whose whips and yokes insult humanity, went into the canvass under the leadership of Douglas, who "did not care whether slavery was voted up or voted down," and of Herschel V. Johnson, who believed that "capital should own labor."

The Republican party, rejecting with horror the wicked dogma that the Constitution of Christian America carried slavery wherever it went, and that the nation's flag protected it wherever it waved, disavowing the abhorrent idea that capital should own labor, caring whether slavery should be voted down or voted up, bravely accepted the.duties imposed upon it by the needs of the country and the providence of Almighty God. Assembling in national convention, it proclaimed that the maintenance of the principle that all men are created equal, is essential to the preservation of our Republican institutions ; that it held in abhorrence all schemes for disunion ; that the dogma that the Constitution carried slavery into the Territories was a dangerous political heresy, revolutionary in its tendency, and that the normal condition of the Territories was that of freedom. Proclaiming, as its faith and creed, this platform, which breathed the vital spirit of freedom, patriotism, justice, and humanity, it presented to the nation Abraham Lincoln, whose name will linger in the hearts and in the memories of men so long as Patriotism and Liberty shall have shrines on earth. (Loud and long-continued applause.)

These two sections of the Democracy, though "distinct like the billows," were yet "one like the sea," in fidelity to the interests of slavery. Though rent and torn, it went into the canvass, appealing to the brutal passions, selfish instincts, and unmanly fears of the country. The leaders of these factions vied with each other in scoffing at the self-evident truths of the Declaration of Independence. Breckinridge, the leader of one faction, pronounced these truths "abstractions," which would "lead our country rapidly to dissolution." Douglas, the chief of the other faction, defined those sublime truths to mean, that "British subjects, on this continent, were equal to British subjects born and residing in Great Britain." Abraham Lincoln pronounced the great truth of that immortal declaration to be "applicable to all men and all times," that "to-day and in all coming days it shall be a rebuke and a stumbling-block to the harbingers of reappearing tyranny and oppression." The Republican party, believing, with its leader, that "this is a world of compensations, and he who would be no slave must consent to have no slave," that "those who deny freedom to others deserve it not for themselves, and, under a just God, can not long retain it," appealed to the people to rally to the standard of imperiled liberty. Nearly two millions of men, regardless of the treasonable menaces and revolutionary teachings of the Democratic leaders, and the ignoble and spiritless submission of the Democratic masses, thronged to the ballot-box, dethroned the slave power, and made Abraham Lincoln President of the United States. (Great cheering.)

South-Carolina, trained for thirty years in the school of treason, leaped headlong into rebellion ; other States quickly followed her example. Then the vaunted Southern Confede-racy, the dream of slave perpetuatists for a generation, rose, on the basis that involuntary servitude was the normal condition of the black race in America. Coming into Congress with official oaths on their perjured lips, these architects of ruin plotted conspiracies in Congress, in the Cabinet, in the Army, in the Navy, everywhere, for the dismemberment of the Union and the death of the nation. The Republic of Washington seemed doomed to a swift and ignominious dissolution—to be stricken from the roll of nations. While these conspirators were organizing treason, seducing the weak, and corrupting the venal, while they were seizing forts, arsenals, arms, and millions of public property, raising batteries for assault or defence, firing upon the old flag, which covered bread for starving soldiers, they were receiving, not the withering, blasting rebukes of insulted patriotism, but aid and comfort from their Northern Democratic associates.

The Democratic President, poor, weak old man, made haste to assure the insurrectionary chiefs that he had arrived at the conclusion "that no power had been delegated to Congress to coerce into submission a State which is attempting to withdraw or which has entirely withdrawn from the confederacy." Attorney-General Black pronounced against the power of the government to coerce a seceding State, and maintained that the attempt to do so "would be an expulsion of such State from the Union," and would absolve all the States "from their Federal obligations," and the people from contributing "their money or their blood to carry on a contest like that." Did not these disorganizing opinions of the President and of the Attorney-General, showing the utter impotency of the imperiled nation, "give aid and comfort" to the conspirators? Did not these sworn guardians of the nation leave the government weaponless, at the mercy of the armed hands of the assassins of the Union?

Jefferson Davis, when he assumed the Presidency of the Confederate government, and proclaimed that "we have entered upon a career of independence, and it must be inflexibly pursued, through many years of controversy, with our late associates of the Northern States," held the written assurance of ex-President Pierce, who believed that the disruption of the Union would not occur without "blood," that "the fighting will not be along Mason and Dixon's line merely, it will be within our own borders, in our own streets." Did not this assurance of Franklin Pierce, that the fighting would be in our streets, between our own citizens, "give aid and comfort" to the rebel President? (Groans for Pierce.)

THE TREASONABLE DEMOCRACY.

Pendleton, who now felicitates himself upon the fact that he imposed his policy, although he could not impose himself, upon the Democratic Convention, declared, in the House of Representatives, in the presence of his Democratic associates, gleefully chuckling over the severed Union, that "armies, money, blood, can not maintain this Union," "the whole scheme of coercion is impracticable," "it is contrary to the genius and the spirit of the Constitution." He, who had never a word of cheer for the loyal, assured the retiring conspirators that "if they must leave the family mansion, I would bid them farewell so tenderly, that they would be forever touched by the recollection." Vallandigham, who has just forced the reluctant Seymour to accept the proffered honors of the New-York Convention, had, in that city, on the eve of the Presidential election, when meditated treason lowered over the country, proclaimed that "if any one of the States should secede, I never would, as a Representative in Congress, vote one dollar whereby one drop of American blood should be shed in civil war." Referring to that early pledge of faithlessness to his country, after armed treason had opened its batteries upon the steamer bearing food to the famishing defenders of beleaguered Sumter, he defiantly said, "I deliberately repeat and reaffirm it, resolved, though I stand alone, though all others yield and fall away, to make it good to the last moment of my official life." Did not that pledge fire the hot blood of the secessionists of South-Carolina? Did not the reaffirming of that unpatriotic declaration excite the hopes and nerve the arms of traitors aiming blows at the nation's life? Did not that pledge, and the reaffirming of that pledge, cause American blood to flow in civil war?

In that time of peril, when the government rocked beneath the blows rained upon it by Democratic traitors; in those days of anxiety and gloom, when the hearts of the loyal throbbed heavily over the sorrows of their betrayed country, there came from Democratic orators, Democratic presses, and Democratic convocations, all over the North, bitter reproaches to loyalty, and words of cheer to disloyalty. From the capital of the Empire State, from that great Democratic Convention at Tweddle Hall, Horatio Seymour sent forth these words, to burden the patriotic men who were maintaining the just power of the government, and to cheer on its deadliest foes: "Let us see if successful coercion by the North is less revolutionary than successful secession by the South." Did not these disorganizing words of Horatio Seymour sadden the country's friend and inspirit the country's enemies? Were not these opinions, pledges, assurances of Buchanan, Black, Pierce, Pendleton, Vallandigham, and Seymour, inspirations to the Southern leaders of secession and disunion? Did they not invite and incite civil war? Does not the blood of our slain sons rest heavily on the souls of our Democratic politicians? Did not these utterances of such exponents of Northern Democracy linger in the memory of Governor Orr, when he said to the men of South-Carolina: "Many of you will remember that, when the war first commenced, great hopes and expectations were held out by our friends in the North and West that there would be no war, and that, if it commenced, it would be north of Mason and Dixon's line, and that it would not be in the South"? Did not Horatio Seymour hold out "great hopes and expectations" to rebels, weaponed with the bullet, in 1861? Does he not now hold out "great hopes and expectations" to Wade Hampton, Forrest, and Robert Toombs, who defiantly declares "as we have no possibility of fighting with the sword, let us fight with the ballot-box"? (A Voice: "Down with the traitors.")

When Southern senators were announcing that the slave States were intending to go out of the Union, that a "Southern confederacy will be formed, and it will be the most successful government in the world," timid conservatism demanded a compromise, by which the nation, by irrepealable constitutional amendments, was to recognize, establish, and protect slavery in the Territories then held, or which might thereafter be acquired South of 36° 30'; to deny power to Congress to abolish slavery in the nation's capital; to allow slave masters and flesh jobbers to take slaves in and through the free States; to take from men of African descent citizenship and suffrage; and to send out of the country, at the expense of the Treasury of the United States, such free negroes as the States might desire to have removed. This most degrading, dishonoring, and humiliating proposition—by far the wickedest proposition ever made in the interests of slavery in America—was, in bitter mockery, christened a "Compromise." This compromise the nation was asked to accept, not to bring South-Carolina and the Gulf States back, but to keep the border States from going out; not to bring pronounced rebels in, but to keep quaking conservatives from going out. Reason and conscience, love of country and of the race, forbade the Republicans in Congress to consummate that crime against the country and its free institutions. They could not, they dared not do so, even under the menaces of a bloody civil war. They feared, if they should change their country from a free to a slaveholding nation, they would live amid the bitter reproaches of a betrayed people, and then sink into dishonored graves with the curses of earth and of Heaven resting upon them forever.

TREASON OF BUCHANAN'S ADMINISTRATION

Day by day, during that terrible winter, the Republicans in Congress, powerless to save, saw with the profoundest sorrow their riven and shattered country sinking into the fathomless abyss of disunion. A Democratic President, a Democratic Attorney-General, had surrendered the life-preserving powers of the government. A Democratic Secretary of the Treasury was deranging the finances and sinking the national credit. A Democratic Secretary of War was scattering the army, and sending muskets, cannon, and the munitions of war to be clutched by rising traitors. A Democratic Secretary of the Interior was permitting the robbery of trust funds, held by the government. A Democratic Secretary of the Navy was rendering that "right arm" of the national service powerless. A Democratic Mayor of the commercial capital of the country was proposing to make that capital a free city, independent of the national government. Democratic leaders were ostentatiously giving pledges "never to vote a man or a dollar" for coercion. Democrats were giving their assurances that regiments, marching to the coercion of the South, "must pass over their dead bodies." Officers of the Senate were members of a secret organization, nightly plotting treason in the capital of the nation. This uprising of traitors, these pledges of Northern Democratic leaders, this submission of the Democratic masses to the plottings of the insurrectionists, rendered more vulgarly insolent the champions of the rebellion at the capital. Sam Houston had not called together the Legislature to hasten Texas out of the Union. Iverson said that if he did not yield to the sentiment of the people, "some Texan Brutus may arise to rid his country of this old, hoary-headed traitor." Mr. Seward invited a calm discussion of the pending issues. Clingman replied that "many of the free debaters were hanging on the trees of Texas." The unarmed " Star of the West," bearing food to defenders of Sumter, was turned back by the frowning batteries of treason. Wigfall tauntingly told us that she had swaggered into Charleston Harbor, had received a stunning blow on the forehead, and staggered out helpless, and we dare not resent it. But in that "dark and troubled night" of Democratic apostasy, Republican hearts were gladdened by the noble fidelity of three Democratic statesmen. In being Democrats, Edwin M. Stanton, Joseph Holt, and John A. Dix did not forget to be patriots. While Horatio Seymour was suddening the hearts of the loyal by his unpatriotic declaration, " Let us see if successful coercion by the North is less revolutionary than successful secession by the South," those same hearts were thrilled by the immortal order of John A. Dix, " If any man hauls down the flag, shoot him."

At last, that long, gloomy, and terrible winter ended, and the fourth of March gladdened the longing eyes and burdened hearts of the patriotic men who clung to their country with deathless tenacity when clouds and darkness were settling upon it. To that day, and to Lincoln, they had looked as anxiously as Wellington, in the crisis of Waterloo, looked " for night or for Blücher." The riven and shattered government passed from the nerveless hand of that weakness which betrayed like treason, into the honest, brave, and strong grasp of Abraham Lincoln. Then that huge, horrid, and barbarizing despotism of the slave propaganda sunk to rise no more. Against that despotism the Republicans had struggled through seven weary years, amid obloquy, reproach, and insult. History would record that, throughout that contest, they had acted in harmony with the Constitution of their country, with the teachings of its illustrious framers, the utterances of poets, sages, and philosophers, and the great and good of all the ages, and with the commands of God's holy word. That stainless record gave assurance to all the world that, in accepting the guardianship of their imperiled country, they would cherish it with all their hearts, and defend it with all their hands. (Long continued cheering.)

THE COMBAT OPENS.

Soon the men to whom the government had been intrusted were summoned to its defense. Mr. Lincoln, in assuming the administration, had proclaimed to his dissatisfied countrymen of the South that " the momentous issues of civil war were in their hands." But the rebel chiefs, fearing that the already aroused passions of the South might not completely sever the bonds of affection ; fearing, too, the effect of the closing words of his inaugural, where, with such pathos, he said, " The mystic chords of memory, stretching from every battle-field and patriot grave, to every living heart and hearthstone all over this broad land, will yet swell the chorus of the Union, when again touched, as they surely will be, by the better angels of our nature," the rebel Secretary of War ordered the batteries menacing Sumter to open their fires upon that devoted fortress. That order was swiftly obeyed. The flag of united America came down, and the confederate flag waved over its smoking ruins. Thus was inaugurated, by Southern Democrats, that great civil war in which 350,000 loyal lives were sacrificed, 400,000 were wounded, $4,000,000,000 were expended, and the productive industries of the country burdened with a national debt of $2,500,000,000. To the full comprehension of every intelligent man in America, whose mind has not been poisoned by our great national crime, nor maddened by partisanship, slavery was the inspiration of this terrible conflict, and the Democratic party its instrument, which must be held responsible, before the present and coming ages, for every drop of blood, and every tear of sorrow, agony, or affection ; for every dollar already expended, and for every dollar of taxation which must, in so many forms, and for so many years, rest heavily on the capital and labor of the country. When any one gazes on the grave of some brave soldier who fell in our defense, upon one wounded in the same stern conflict, or upon the vacant chairs around the hearthstones of the land ; whenever he is called to contribute to the relief of the wives and children of our slain countrymen ; whenever he reads the tax list, or pays, in some of its various forms, his portion of our vast taxation, let him not forget that all this is due to the apostasy of the Democratic party—to the open treason of its Davises, Toombs, and Masons of the South, and the ill-concealed sympathy of the Pierces, the Seymours, the Pendletons, and their many other partisans at the North.

· THE UPRISING OF THE PEOPLE.

The Republican administration promptly accepted "the momentous issues of civil war," thus forced upon it. The President immediately issued a call for 75,000 men to protect the capital ; which was followed, in a few days, by another for 300,000. for the suppression of the Rebellion. On the 4th of July, Congress assembled, gave the President 500,000 men and $500,000,000, and adopted the requisite legislation for the organization and government of the military forces of the United States. The uprising of the people, startled by the echoes of the cannon which treason trained on Sumter, had silenced the rebel-sympathizing Democracy. Little was now heard against " coercion ;" but Breckinridge, who yet lingered in the Senate, and Powell, Pendleton,

Cox, Vallandigham, and their Democratic associates protested against "the subjugation of the South." The Administration, sustained by Congress, the united Republican party, and many patriotic men of the Democratic and other political organizations in the nation, raised and sent into the field more than 2,000,-000 men, created the most powerful navy that ever rode the ocean, fought six hundred actions upon land and sea, "coerced" rebel States, "subjugated" the South, destroyed or captured the rebel armies, and utterly annihilated the power of the Confederate government ; so that a rebel bayonet no longer gleamed in the Southern sun, nor a rebel banner waved on the Southern breeze.

LOYAL DEMOCRATS FOR THE COUNTRY.

In the grand uprising of the people, after the firing upon Sumter, many Democrats who had followed the lead of Buchanan, Pierce, Seymour, Pendleton, and their compeers, nobly atoned for the past by consecrating themselves, all they were and all they hoped to be, to their country. During these seven years of trial, in the field and in the councils of the nation, they have associated their names forever with the defenders of the country and the champions of liberty ; but most of the leaders of the Democracy bowed rather than yielded to the patriotic current that swept over the land. Poisoned by slavery, dominated so long by the slave power and the chiefs of the rebellion, they trusted that the disappointments, losses, and sacrifices of the war would bring a reaction, and that their hour of triumph would soon come. General John Cochrane, who well knew these Democratic leaders, said, in a letter written from the swamps of the Chickahominy, in the early summer of 1862 : "They will emerge from their gloom as the shadows fall upon their country." The shadows soon fell upon the country. Disasters came to our armies. The disappointments and sacrifices of the war, and Mr. Lincoln's Proclamation of Emancipation, hastened the hoped-for reaction. State after State pronounced against the Administration. In their triumphs the Democratic leaders indulged in words and acts showing unmistakably to all the world that they regarded the government of the United States and Abraham Lincoln, not the government of the confederacy and Jefferson Davis, their foes. So unpatriotic were the legislatures of Indiana and Illinois that Governor Morton and Governor Yates were forced to prorogue them and send the conspirators to their homes. Democratic orators, presses, and societies, all over the North, assailed the Administration, struggling to suppress the rebellion, in language so violent, seditious, and revolutionary, that it gave confidence to the rebel councils and hope to the rebel armies. Horatio Seymour, elected in the disastrous autumn of 1862 governor of New-York, over the patriotic and self-sacrificing Wadsworth, professing to speak for a dissatisfied people, burdened by word and act the great heart of Abraham Lincoln. To this carping and fault-finding governor, Mr. Lincoln sent the very significant message, that "if he wants to be President of the United States,

he had better unite with me in preserving the United States, to be president of."

THE VALLANDIGHAM AND PENDLETON GANG.

Exhaustive marches and decimating battles thinned the armies that carried upon their glittering bayonets the faith of the Republic. Their wasting ranks must be refilled with the fresh blood of heroic manhood. The exhausting demands, early made on the country, the pressing wants and high rewards of labor, checked enlistments. To fill the ranks of the country's defenders, to equalize the burdens of war between the States and sections of the same States, the thirty-seventh Congress, in its closing hours, passed an "Act for enrolling and calling out the national forces." In passing that great measure, the Republicans in Congress believed it would revive the drooping heart of the people, fill the wasting ranks of our battalions, carry dismay into the councils of treason, and give assurance to the nations of the earth that the American people had that spirit of personal sacrifice and heroic endeavor which would insure the unity of the Republic and the perpetuity of the nation. But, unmindful of the pressing needs of the bleeding country, the Democrats fiercely opposed its enactment. Vallandigham, pledged to vote neither men nor money, denounced it as a measure "to abrogate the Constitution, and erect upon the ruins of civil and political liberty a stupendous structure of despotism." Pendleton and Voorhees joined in its denunciation. Cox would prevent the enrolling of black men to fight the battles of the endangered country. Democratic orators and presses, open and secret societies, united in assailing a measure that enabled the government to command the entire resources of the nation for its defense. Fernando Wood and his Mozart tribe, the crafty but irresolute Seymour, instilled into the too credulous ear of ignorance poisonous words, inflaming its heart and maddening its brain, till Murder, clutching its weapon, and Arson, seizing its brand, reddened the pavements of New-York with blood and illumined her streets with the flames of burning asylums. ("Down with Seymour!") When we consider these reckless utterances of men who denied our right to coerce States or "subjugate the South," the treasonable organizations of the "Knights of the Golden Circle" and "Sons of Liberty," in the West, the speeches of Democratic politicians who, throughout the war, never uttered a word that could be tortured into meaning that the rebel government, rebel armies, and rebel people, were their enemies or the enemies of their country, we do not wonder that rebel chiefs and rebel presses, even after Lee's army had been hurled back from the glorious field of Gettysburg, Vicksburg had surrendered to Grant, and Port Hudson to Banks, and the waters of the Mississippi to the sea reflected the stars of the national flag, boastfully proclaimed that "the gore of Lincoln's hated minions wets the streets," that the government is "cowering," and that "the days as well as the soldiers of the Federal army are numbered." (Great applause.)

WISDOM OF CONGRESS AND PATRIOTISM OF THE PEOPLE.

The Republican Administration had not only to create armies and navies, but to perform the far more difficult task of providing the vast resources to sustain a conflict so gigantic. It established internal revenue systems, revised the revenue laws, and established a national banking system. The Republicans may have committed some mistakes in the *details* of their financial policy, but the success of that policy is the marvel of men the world over. Its wonderful success falsified the predictions of financial men in the old world and in the new. Democrats have carped at it, criticised it, misapprehended it, and misrepresented it. Many of them predicted that the bonds of the government would never be redeemed, refused to purchase them themselves, or advise their friends to do so, and are presenting now a fitting sequel to their early and persistent opposition, by their seeming anxiety and efforts to prove their ill-omened predictions true. Horatio Seymour has it authoritatively announced that he does not own and never has owned one of the bonds of the government. He is known to be a man of large wealth, and to have inherited a fortune. During years of the war the country owed hundred of millions to tho army it could not pay. The heroes of Gettysburg and Vicksburg had gone months without payment; often the government was in debt five and six months, and sometimes more, to our soldiers. Brave men received and read to their comrades, around their camp-fires, letters from their wives, begging for money to keep themselves and their children from want. Men who faced shot and shell in the field, were unmanned and wept like children in their tents over letters received from their homes, because of this poverty of the national treasury. Was it not, then, as patriotic to loan money to the government to feed and clothe the country's defenders, and keep their wives and children from want, as it was to confront that country's enemies on the field of battle? Patriotic men, and women, too, in all the conditions of life, loaned money to the government, often to their own inconvenience and disadvantage, to support and pay those who were bleeding and dying in its defense. And yet the Democratic party has become so demoralized by blind, unreasoning partisanship, that Horatio Seymour, its candidate for the presidency, to strengthen himself with the men of his party, who would impair the credit and repudiate the obligations of the government, incurred for its salvation, has it authoritatively announced that he has not now, and never had, a single bond, though given for a purpose so sacred, and to avert a peril so extreme. When hundreds of thousands of our brave soldiers were unpaid for months, leaving, of course, their wives and children to great inconvenience, if not to absolute and extreme suffering, often to be relieved by the hand of charity, because the government could not borrow money to meet these most imperious claims, he, though abounding in wealth of his own, and the almoner of that of others, had not a dollar for those heroic men fighting his battles, nor for their starving families, suffering for the same great cause. This announcement of Horatio Seymour, that he did not lend his money to the government in the hour of its extreme need is a cowardly and unpatriotic avowal, which should bring to him, not the suffrages and honors of the people, but their blasting rebukes and withering scorn. The "Knights of the Golden Circle," the "Sons of Liberty," the holders of the bonds of the Confederate government, the men, North and South, who, in the language of a son of Maryland, "would not pay the bondholders because the money was loaned for the wicked purpose of fighting our Southern brethren," may applaud this boastful announcement; but the patriotic men, and the men whose wives and children were the victims of his unpatriotic action, will applaud him never. (Applause, and cries of "No, never.")

When the Legal Tender Act was pending in the House of Representatives, Pendleton, now nicknamed "Young Greenbacks," declared that these legal tender notes would go out to the country "with the mark of Cain upon them;" that they would be "wanderers and vagabonds" in the land;" and wherever they wandered, they would carry bankruptcy and repudiation. Evils are indeed inseparable from paper money. But the benefits to the country of that Legal Tender Act during the war can never be overestimated. Pendleton, who led in opposition to its adoption, as a temporary measure, in times of dire necessity—he who deemed "greenbacks " "wanderers and vagabonds," with the "mark of Cain " upon them—assumes the championship now of a system so modified, that his prediction, that they would lead to bankruptcy and repudiation, may be realized. (A voice: "Oh! he is played out.")

TRIUMPHS OF THE REPUBLICAN PARTY.

For many years the toiling millions demanded that the public domain should be withheld from the hard grasp of the speculator, and granted, in limited quantities, to actual settlers. This demand, of land for the landless, of small farms tilled by men standing on their own acres, was made in the interests of freedom, culture, development, and Christian civilization. It was the idea of the farm against the plantation—of free labor against slave labor —of the perennial verdure of liberty against the blight and mildew of slavery. The slavemasters of the great plantations, the accepted leaders of the Democracy, were as sternly opposed to the policy of small farms and "land for the landless " as they were to "free soil " for free labor. The Republican party coming into power, the representative of this policy of free soil for free labor—of the farm against the plantation—of land for the landless—consecrated all the public domain to freedom, and, by legislative enactments, set apart more than a thousand million of acres as homesteads for actual settlers. To the Republican party are the landless toilers of our country indebted for this beneficent system—this splendid inheritance for themselves and their posterity.

Judge the Republican party, during its seven years of power, by its deeds; test it by its defense and protection of the nation against the most gigantic conspiracy of ancient or modern times, by its development of the nation's power and the advancement of its material interests, and it stands on a higher plane than that of any political organization on the globe.

But grander far than the raising of armies and the creation of navies, than marches or sieges or battles on land or wave, was the far-reaching, comprehensive, and crowning deed of emancipation. That huge, hideous, and horrid system of human bondage in Christian America, upheld by the aggregated interest of $3,000,000,000 in the flesh and blood, brain and soul of man, hedged about by the accumulated passions and prejudices, prides and ambitions of seven generations, intrenched within the social, political, and ecclesiastical organizations and affiliations of life, was shivered to atoms by the blows, sturdy and persistent, of the Republican party. By a series of executive and legislative acts, it broke the chains and lifted from the depths of chattelhood up to the summits of manhood four and a half millions of beings made in the image of God. It was said of Wilberforce that he went to God with the shackles of eight hundred thousand West-India slaves in his hands. The Republican party enters the forum of the nations with four and a half millions of riven fetters in one hand, and four and a half million of title-deeds of American citizenship in the other. These broken fetters—these title-deeds—it holds up to the gaze of the living present and the advancing future. In the progress of the ages it has been given to few generations, in any form or by any modes, to achieve a work so vast, so grand, so sure to be recorded by the historic pen or flung upon the canvas in enduring colors. Defeat and disaster may come upon the Republican party—it may perish utterly from the land it saved and made free—but its name will be forever associated with the emancipation of millions of a poor, friendless, and hated race, their elevation to the heights of citizenship, their exaltation to equality of civil rights and privileges, and, crowning act of all, the prerogative " to vote and to be voted for." These beneficent deeds will live in the hearts of coming generations, and "brighter glow and gleam immortal, unconsumed by moth or rust." (Cheers.)

THE DISGRACED DEMOCRACY.

In this grand work, applauded by earth and blest of heaven, the Democratic party had no part whatever. For more than a quarter of a century, before slavery raised the banners of civil war, it had been its pliant tool, ever swift to come to its support before it was called, and run on its errands before it was sent. Ever prompt to obey its decrees, the Democracy clung to the relentless and unappeasable foe of the country after that foe had inspired a bloody revolution to blot the North-American Republic from the map of nations. After civil war had reddened the bright waters and green fields with the blood of our slain sons—after it had sent wounds, sickness, and sorrows into the homes of the people—the Democratic party persistently continued to resist every measure

for the nation's defense, if that measure tended, in the slightest degree, to weaken the admitted cause of all our woe. Throughout the war, of which slavery was the inspiration, the heart, and soul, and long after it became clear to the comprehension of intelligent patriotism that its death would be the annihilation of the rebellion, the unity of the Republic, the life of the nation, the harmonious development of free institutions, the repose, culture, and renown of the people, the Democratic party mourned, and would not be comforted, over every blow struck at the retreating fiend. (Sensation.)

As during the seven years from 1854 to 1861, when in possession of power, so during the seven years from 1861 to 1868, when out of power, the Democratic party has been the deadliest foe of the African race and of its friends. It has scoffed at, and jeered at, every generous, humane, and ennobling idea, and steadfastly striven to defeat every measure to make it free, recognize its rights, or elevate its condition. It resisted making free slaves used by rebels for military purposes at the opening of the war, and the act forbidding officers of the army to return fugitives seeking the protection of the national flag—the abolition of slavery in the nation's capital and the prohibition of slavery in the national Territories—the repeal of the Fugitive Slave Act and the freedom of slaves captured' or coming within the lines of our armies—the recognition of the nationality of Hayti and Liberia, and Mr. Lincoln's Proclamation of Emancipation—the enrollment of black soldiers to fight the battles of the country and the freedom of black soldiers, their wives and their children—the admission of the colored people of the District of Columbia to the right to testify in the courts and to the right to ride in the public conveyances—the constitutional amendment forever abolishing slavery in the United States, and the Freedmen's Bureau for the aid, protection, and education of emancipated bondsmen—suffrage to colored men in the District of Columbia and in the Territories of the United States—the Civil Rights measure, securing to black men the full and equal benefit of all laws for the security of person and property, and the amendment to the Constitution, providing that no person shall be denied equal protection of the laws equalizing representation, so that three of Wade Hampton's troopers shall no longer count the same as seven of the loyal soldiers of the North, and forbidding the payment of the rebel debt or payment for slaves emancipated — the Reconstruction measure, giving to colored men in rebel States the right to vote, and the acts for restoring the seven reconstructed States to their practical relations to the government. During all the struggles for these and kindred measures, by which slavery has been abolished and the freedmen elevated to the full rights and privileges of American citizenship in the States lately in rebellion, the Democratic party has appealed and now appeals to the basest passions and prejudices, still to oppress this people and hinder the realization of their new-born hopes inspired by emancipation. To keep them in bondage and still to prevent their development, it has studiously misrepresented the sentiments, opinions, and acts of their friends. No character however pure, no services however exalted, could preserve any man, or set of men, from their obloquy, foul abuse, and viperous malignity. ("That is true."

THE CHICAGO REBEL CONVENTION.

In 1864, when Grant was holding Lee in his grasp in the rebel capital, and Sherman was fighting his bloody way to Atlanta, when patriot hearts were cheered by the hope of soon subjugating the rebellion, the Democratic party assembled at Chicago. Horatio Seymour presided. The convention, inspired by slavery and in sympathy with their rebel Democratic friends in rebellion, resolved that the "war is a failure," and demanded "the cessation of hostilities." The Republican party met in convention, declared for the complete abolition of slavery, the subjugation of the rebellion, and the reëlection of Abraham Lincoln. These two parties, numbering more than four millions of voters, went to the ballot-box. The Republicans invoked the patriotism, the love of liberty, and the self-sacrificing spirit of the country. The Democrats appealed to cowardly fears, selfish instincts, and unreasoning passions and prejudices. The Democracy, boastful as is its wont, received 21 out of 234 electoral votes, and was beaten by a popular majority of more than 400,000 votes. The spirit of the rebellion was thus broken. The hopes of the rebel chiefs, excited by Democratic assurances, were crushed, and, in a few months, the rebel armies surrendered to our advancing legions. (Long continued and vociferous cheering.)

ANOTHER STRUGGLE.

In November there is to be another struggle between these two parties for the control of the national administration. The Republican party met at Chicago, reaffirmed its policy of reconstruction, pronounced against all forms of repudiation, for the reduction and equalization of taxation, for the equal protection of American citizens, for the recognized obligations to our soldiers, and to the widows and orphans, of the gallant dead, and for the removal of restrictions imposed upon rebels as rapidly as the safety of the loyal people will admit. The convention then presented the name of General Grant, the great captain who has so often marshaled our armies to victory; and Schuyler Colfax, a statesman of pure life, stainless honor, and commanding influence

THE NEW-YORK REBEL CONVENTION.

The Democratic party assembled in national convention in New-York. Horatio Seymour again presided. That selection of its presiding officer was a monition to the country that this convention would be no more patriotic or wise than was the Democratic convention of 1864. There assembled the self-same leaders, or their compeers, that pronounced, in 1864, the war, to preserve the nation's life, "a failure," and demanded "a cessation of hostilities," which would have made inevitable a dismemberment of the Republic and the death of the

nation. To that convention came also a few disappointed, sour, and fallen spirits, who once were enlisted with the legions of Liberty, but who were never imbued with the generous and ennobling impulses of Human Equality. There came, too, the exponents and representatives of the "lost cause." These representatives were not the men whose eyes had been opened in the storm of civil war to see the error of secession, and who had repented of their treason against the best government in the world—treason made in the interest of the wickedest rebellion in history—a rebellion recognizing slavery as the normal condition of society in Christian America and the corner-stone of their new government. These were the men in whose bosoms still burned the aggressive and dominating spirit of oppression and caste. These were the men who, with no change of feeling, sentiment, or purpose, came to retrieve in the arena of politics what they had lost on the field of battle. There was Wade Hampton, of South-Carolina, who, on his way to the convention, said to the students of General Lee's college, "The cause for which Stonewall Jackson fell, can not be in vain, but in some form will yet triumph." There was Gov. Vance, of North-Carolina, who told rebel troops, during the war, to "pile hell so full of Yankees that their feet will stick out of the windows." There was Buckner, of Kentucky, who came to Washington, at the opening of the war, to procure arms for his State and a commission for himself; but who went back to Kentucky, betrayed his State and country, joined the rebel ranks, and was afterward forced to surrender "unconditionally" to Gen. Grant. There was Preston, also of Kentucky, who abandoned his State, became a rebel general, a commissioner and conspirator in Europe, against his country. There was Basil Duke, one of John Morgan's lieutenants in his thieving, robbing, and murderous raids through Ohio and Indiana. There was Robert Ould, of Virginia, rebel general and commissioner, and familiar with the horrors of Belle Isle and Libby Prison. There was Forrest, of Fort Pillow infamy, concerning whose fiendish conduct a Congressional committee thus reports: "Of the men, from 300 to 400 are known to have been killed at Fort Pillow, of whom at least THREE HUNDRED *were murdered in cold blood after the post was in possession of the rebels, and our men had thrown down their arms and ceased to offer resistance.*" Of 182 members of the convention, from the rebel States, there was not one Union man of well-known and approved loyalty. There were more rebel soldiers than soldiers of the Union army—more members of Jeff Davis's Congress than of the Congress of the United States. Is there any wonder, then, that one, who had heard the rebel battle *yell* in the land of the rebellion, should have instinctively exclaimed, "the rebel yell," as he heard the shout that arose at the words of Wade Hampton's resolution, declaring the Reconstruction Acts "revolutionary, unconstitutional, and void"?

THE YOUNG GREENBACK'S SWINDLE.

The financial portion of the Democratic platform was dictated by Pendleton. That great financial genius seems to be hugely pleased with his work. It is, however, a cheat, a delusion, and a snare. The government owes a bonded debt paying interest, and a non paying interest debt. If this platform means that the government shall redeem the bonds with the greenback debt, now issued, then it is a simple swindle, for the government has none of its greenback debt to use for that purpose. If it is meant that the government, in violation of its pledge, shall issue more of its non-interest paying debts to redeem the interest-bearing debt, then it means a further depreciated currency, the derangement of legitimate business, the robbery of honest labor, ruinous losses, bankruptcy, and ultimate repudiation. (Many voices: "That's true doctrine.")

A REBEL MAKES THE PLATFORM.

Wade Hampton claims the honor of having constructed so much of the platform, touching reconstruction, etc., as declares it to be "revolutionary, unconstitutional, and void." In a speech to the men of South-Carolina, he says: "I said I would take the resolutions if they would allow me to add but three words, which you will find embodied in the platform. I added this: 'And we declare that the reconstruction acts are revolutionary, unconstitutional, and void.' When I proposed that, every single member of the committee—and the warmest men in it were the men of the North —came forward and said they would carry it out to the end." The committee on the platform and the convention accept from Wade Hampton this declaration, and they pledge themselves to carry it out to the end. What that "end" is to be, is embodied in this declaration of their candidate for the vice-presidency. In his letter which secured his nomination, Mr. Blair says: "There is but one way to restore the government and the constitution, and that is to declare the reconstruction acts null and void, compel the army to undo its usurpations at the South, disperse the carpet-bag State governments, and allow the white people to reorganize their own governments and elect senators and representatives. We must have a president who will execute the will of the people by trampling into dust the usurpations of Congress known as the reconstruction acts. I wish to stand before the convention upon this issue, as it is one which embraces everything else that is of value in its large and comprehensive results."

REBEL OPINIONS.

The platform having been constructed, the persuasive Vallandigham overcame the scruples of the coyish Seymour, who consented to be "caught by the whirling tide." Under the lead of Preston, Hampton, and Forest, the convention associated the dashing Blair with the timorous Seymour. This disunion platform, declaring the reconstruction of seven States and their representation in Congress "revolutionary, unconstitutional, and void"—this ticket, pledged to "declare the reconstruction acts null and void, compel the army to undo its usurpations, disperse the carpet-bag State governments, and allow the white people to reorganize their own governments and elect senators and representatives"—is indorsed by the Northern Democracy with the same cordiality with which they indorsed the platform of 1864, declaring "the war a failure," and demanding "the cessation of hostilities." Southern Democrats, who could not indorse the Democratic platform of 1864, or support its ticket, because three quarters of a million of "boys in blue" stood between them and their Northern friends, could leap over the graves of three hundred and fifty thousand dead heroes, and fraternally embrace their sympathizing friends, who have ever maintained that the government could not "coerce a State" or "subjugate the South," and indorse platform and ticket. Henry A. Wise proclaims that "secession is more alive than ever," and he supports Seymour and Blair because they will "assume military power" for the overthrow of the reconstructed governments of the South. Vance boasted to the people of Richmond, on his way home from the New-York convention, that "the South would gain by the election of Seymour and Blair all it fought for in the rebellion." Admiral Semmes, who commanded the Alabama when the Kearsarge, in the face of Europe, sent her to the bottom of the seas, and who revenged himself by destroying unarmed Yankee whalers after the rebellion had been subdued, said, in a ratification speech at Mobile: "I have been a Democrat all my life, before the war, during the war, and since the war, and fought the war on the principles of the Democracy. . . . The grand old Democratic party has arisen from its long slumber —and the election of Seymour and Blair will reduce the negro to a subordinate position as an inferior race." Percy Walker told the same Mobile assemblage that this is the first time, since Lee tendered to the enemy that sword which "flashed victoriously over so many battle-fields, that I have seen a light on the clouds hanging over the South;" for "the great Democratic party has taken up our cause." Robert Toombs, who went into the rebellion for the right to call the roll of his slaves on Bunker Hill, and came out of the rebellion without the right to call that roll on his own plantation, vauntingly proclaimed to the Democracy of Georgia, gathered in mass convention at Atlanta, that, "as the late war was produced by the *defeated* Democratic party in '60, we shall never have peace till it is *restored* in '68." He divines the mission of the party, for he tells the delighted Georgians that "the grinning skeletons which have been set up in our midst as legislators shall be ousted by Frank Blair, whom the Democratic party has expressly appointed for that purpose. All these things shall be swept from the bosom of the country." Howell Cobb, denouncing Governor Brown, the loyal white men of Georgia, and repentant rebels and loyal men, who are honestly striving to secure peace, order, and law, as traitors to the country, thus characterizes and counsels concerning them: "You owe it to the living, you owe it to your own children and to their children. Write down in their memories this day and all days and for all time to come *the feeling and spirit of abhorrence with which you regard and estimate these men.* O Heaven! for some blistering words that I may write infamy upon the forehead of these men; that they may travel through earth despised of all men and rejected of heaven, scorned by the devil himself. They may seek their final congenial resting-place under the mudsills of that ancient institution." This reconstructed Democrat is the same Howell Cobb, of whom Andrew Johnson said: "Cobb remained in the Cabinet until the treasury was bankrupt and the national credit disgraced at home and abroad, and then he conscientiously seceded."

THE KU-KLUX DEMOCRACY.

These are but specimen utterances which unrepentant and Southern Democratic politicians are pouring into the too willing ear of the people of the South, lately in rebellion against their country. The declaration of General Blair, in favor of trampling in the dust the Reconstruction Acts, instantly aroused the rebel element of the South and sent the *Ku-Klux Klans* on their errands of insult, outrage and death. No wonder that the rebel Gen. Preston hastened to nominate the author of that rebel-inspiring letter as the candidate for the Vice-Presidency; no wonder that Wade Hampton leaped to the floor to second the nomination; no wonder that Fort Pillow Forrest, who now declares that, in a certain event, he will "toot his horn" for the rising of his "old troopers," and who, as at Fort Pillow, will "give no quarter," announced with so much unction the vote of Tennessee. Blair's disorganizing, seditious, and revolutionary letter struck a responsive chord in the bosoms of the Southern Democratic leaders. These delegates assured their Northern political associates that they could carry the reconstructed States for the greenback and grayback ticket. The bolder of the rebel leaders hardly disguise their purpose to seize the polls and have only the white vote cast and counted. Wade Hampton called on his Democratic associates in New-York to "register an oath" that they would place Seymour and Blair in the White House, if they received the majority of white votes, "in spite of all the bayonets that can be brought against them." This rebel trooper and Democratic leader tells the people of the South "not to employ any one, white or black, who gives his aid to the Republican party." And this proposition is generally approved and applauded by Southern politicians and presses, though so cruel and oppressive to the poor laboring men, houseless and homeless, who will thus be compelled to exercise the right of suffrage under duress, and with the menace constantly before them of being driven from their humble cabins and dispossessed even of the fields they are cultivating on shares.

A RESULT OF REPUBLICAN SUCCESS.

I need dwell but briefly on what the Republican party proposes to do. Its history, its platform, and its candidates speak to the full comprehension of the American people. To that history, to that platform, and to those can-

didates it points with confidence and pride. It appeals, as ever, to the higher and better sentiments and impulses of the nation. (Applause.) It appeals to that comprehensive patriotism, which embraces the whole country and the people of the whole country, to that love of liberty which accords equal rights to all men, to that sense of justice that gives equal protection to the poor man's cabin and the rich man's mansion, and to that humanity that lifts up the lowly and the weak. If success crowns its efforts, if the administration shall be intrusted to General Grant, with a House of Representatives to sustain that administration, the policy of reconstruction will be perfected, the States will all be speedily restored to their practical relations to the general government, equal rights will be assured and disabilities removed, the nation's faith will be untarnished, its currency and credit improved, and "Peace," in the language of Mr. Lincoln, "will come to stay." Then the blood, poured out like autumnal rains, will not have been shed in vain; for then united and free America, with liberty for all and justice to all, will enter upon a career of development, culture, and progress, that shall insure a "future grand and great." (Loud cheering.)

THE TRAITOROUS DEMOCRACY.

No less significant and no less pronounced are the history, the platform, and the candidates of the Democratic party. Its history recalls no inspiring ideas, no beneficent policies, no ennobling deeds for patriotism, for liberty, for justice, and for humanity. But it does recall images of slavery—its shackles, its whips, its unrequited toils and its all-pervading impurities — the slave power, its arrogant dominations and aggressive demands, ever associated with humiliating concessions, compromises and apostasies to freedom; dark conspiracies, lawless rebellion, fields of blood, taxation, debts, and the graves of the nation's dead. Its platform speaks of the Reconstruction Acts as "revolutionary, unconstitutional, and void,"—beneficent acts by which seven disorganized commonwealths were reorganized on the basis of loyalty and liberty, and restored to representation in Congress and to the blessings and benefits of the Union. Its candidates are pledged to "trample in the dust those reorganized and restored commonwealths, their constitutions and laws, by which equal rights and privileges are accorded and secured to all. Those candidates are also pledged for that unconstitutional, un-American, and wicked monstrosity, so alien in spirit and tone to the Declaration of Independence and the utterances of the fathers, "*a White Man's Government,*" in place of the constitutional and American idea—a government "of all, by all, for all." This record of fourteen years, this platform, and these candidates, the wild, revolutionary, and disorganizing utterances of Blair, Toombs, Cobb, and other Southern Democratic leaders, speak, in language not to be misunderstood by the country, the purposes of the Democratic party, and WHAT IT PROPOSES TO DO. The currency is to be farther depreciated; the public faith broken, and the national honor tainted; State constitutions are to be abrogated; the civil rights of millions impaired; the right to vote, now a possession, taken from three fourths of a million of working-men; the education of the people, so longed for by the poor of both races, is to be postponed; hatreds, insults, and outrages to the loyal are to be intensified; the soldier, who fought for the restoration of the seceding States, and who now hopes, by his skilled industry, to make the war-wasted fields of the South bloom once more, is to be forced to leave his new home, and the malignant spirit of slavery and caste is to rule again. Then this murderous advice of Albert Pike, the friend and champion of Blair and Seymour, addressed to the young men of Mississippi, may be accepted and followed to "the bitter end":

"Young men, it is for you to bring back to the country its golden days. The South is our land. The North is a foreign and hostile realm. Stand at the altar of your country. Swear eternal hatred to its oppressors. Swear that the day shall come when the Susquehanna and Ohio shall be like rivers of fire, as they are now rivers of blood, between your native land and that of the northern Huns, which no man shall attempt to cross and live."

CONCLUSION.

With one or the other of these two great parties, fellow-citizens, you are constrained to act in the coming election of a President of the United States. Consider well, I pray you, the histories, the platforms, and candidates of these parties now asking your suffrages. Remember that by its fruits the tree is known, and by his deeds man is judged. Apply to these political organizations those words of Holy Writ. Test them by the high standards of love of country and love of man, and vote as they prompt and approve. So voting, you shall do something to heal the wounds of war, rebuke and repress lawlessness and violence, develop the material and moral forces of the land, secure equality of rights and privileges, and thus lift our country to its predestined rank among the nations. (Long-continued cheering.)

PLATFORM

REPUBLICAN PARTY.

THE following Platform, reported by the Committee on Resolutions, was unanimously adopted by the National Republican Convention at Chicago:

First. We congratulate the country on the assured success of the reconstruction policy of Congress, as evinced by the adoption, in a majority of the States lately in rebellion, of constitutions securing equal civil and political rights to all, and regard it as the duty of the Government to sustain those constitutions, and to prevent the people of such States from being remitted to a state of anarchy or military rule.

Second. The guarantee by Congress of equal suffrage to all loyal men at the South was demanded by every consideration of public safety, of gratitude, and of justice, and must be maintained; while the question of suffrage in all the loyal States properly belongs to the people of those States.

Third. We denounce all forms of repudiation as a national crime, and national honor requires the payment of the public indebtedness in the utmost good faith to all creditors at home and abroad not only according to the letter, but the spirit of the laws under which it was contracted.

Fourth. It is due to the labor of the nation that taxation should be equalized and reduced as rapidly as the national faith will permit.

Fifth. The national debt, contracted as it has been for the preservation of the Union for all time to come, should be extended over a fair period for redemption; and it is the duty of Congress to reduce the rate of interest thereon, whenever it can honestly be done.

Sixth. That the best policy to diminish our burden of debt is to so improve our credit that capitalists will seek to loan us money at lower rates of interest than we now pay, and must continue to pay so long as repudiation, partial or total, open or covert, is threatened or suspected.

Seventh. The Government of the United States should be administered with the strictest economy; and the corruptions which have been so shamefully nursed and fostered by Andrew Johnson call loudly for radical reform.

Eighth. We profoundly deplore the untimely and tragic death of Abraham Lincoln, and regret the accession of Andrew Johnson to the Presidency, who has acted treacherously to the people who elected him and the cause he was pledged to support; has usurped high legislative and judicial functions; has refused to execute the laws; has used his high office to induce other officers to ignore and violate the laws; has employed his executive powers to render insecure the property, peace, liberty, and life of the citizen; has abused the pardoning power; has denounced the National Legislature as unconstitutional; has persistently and corruptly resisted, by every means in his power, every proper attempt at the reconstruction of the States lately in rebellion; has perverted the public patronage into an engine of wholesale corruption, and has been justly impeached for high crimes and misdemeanors, and properly pronounced guilty thereof by the votes of thirty-five Senators.

Ninth. The doctrine of Great Britain and other European powers, that because a man is once a subject he is always so, must be resisted at every hazard by the United States as a relic of the feudal times not authorized by the law of nations and at war with our national honor and independence. Naturalized citizens are entitled to be protected in all their rights of citizenship as though they were native born, and no citizen of the United States, native or naturalized, must be liable to arrest and imprisonment by any foreign power for acts done or words spoken in this country. And if so arrested and imprisoned, it is the duty of the Government to interfere in his behalf.

Tenth. Of all who were faithful in the trials of the late war, there were none entitled to more especial honor than the brave soldiers and seamen who endured the hardships of campaign and cruize, and imperiled their lives in the service of the country. The bounties and pensions provided by law for these brave defenders of the nation are obligations never to be forgotten. The widows and orphans of the gallant dead are the wards of the people, a sacred legacy bequeathed to the nation's protecting care.

Eleventh. Foreign emigration, which in the past has added so much to the wealth, development of resources, and increase of power of this nation, "the asylum of the oppressed of all nations," should be fostered and encouraged by a liberal and just policy.

Twelfth. This Convention declares its sympathy with all the oppressed peoples who are struggling for their rights.

On motion of General Carl Schurz, the following additional resolutions were unanimously adopted as part of the platform :

Resolved, That we highly commend the spirit of magnanimity and forbearance with which the men who have served in the rebellion, but now frankly and honestly coöperate with us in restoring the peace of the country and reconstructing the Southern State governments upon the basis of impartial justice and equal rights, are received back into the communion of the loyal people; and we favor the removal of the disqualifications and restrictions imposed upon the late rebels in the same measure as the spirit of disloyalty will die out, and as may be consistent with the safety of the loyal people.

Resolved, That we recognize the great principles laid down in the immortal Declaration of Independence as the true foundation of democratic government, and we hail with gladness every effort toward making these principles a living reality on every inch of American soil.